MAKING
TRUST
HAPPEN!

HOW TO THINK
AND TALK ABOUT
TRUST

& EXPERIENCE
AND CREATE IT

A REFERENCE MANUAL

Jerome S. Paige | Cynthia O. Pace

"Recast the familiar until it demands explanation."

Life's Little Deconstruction Book #321

Self-Help for the Post-Hip

Table of Contents

Making Happen...

"Think outside the box!"

Easier said than done.

Why?

We often don't know "the box" we're thinking inside of.

We can't name what names us.

We don't know our "known worlds."

Our "Making Happen Series" helps us construct and deconstruct our frames of reference, provides us a view of our "boxes," inside and out, and assists us in "making sense" of our feelings and experiences as we seek new ways to engage ourselves, others, our organizations, and our world.

"Making Trust Happen" is the first publication in our series. Future topics include peace, wealth/poverty, racism/anti-racism, and self-regard.

About Our Reference Manual for Our Model T

Who's Our Reference Manual For?

We developed our *Reference Manual* for facilitators. Like many, we realize that when "trust appears," team relationships strengthen. Team members no longer spend time second-guessing one another, and life in our organizations is more comfortable.

When "trust happens," ***ease of being*** permeates our organizations and us as well.

"How do we make trust happen and create that ease of being?"

We contemplate this question.

As we ponder it, we'll:

1. Find that **trust** has an "ineffable" quality. "You-know-it-when-you-see-it" or "don't-see-it." It's ineffable because it "co-appears" with self-trusting, trusting, trustworthiness, trust relationships, and trust structures. "Trust" has no independent existence.

2. Explore how these five dimensions of trust interact to create a sixth one, systemic trust.

3. Discover that trust's elusiveness dissipates once we understand its V + 1 perspectives.

4. Learn tools to think and talk about "trust" and how to experience and create it.

Who's Our Reference Manual For?

We developed our *Reference Manual* for facilitators. Like many, we realize that when "trust appears," team relationships strengthen. Team members no longer spend time second-guessing one another, and life in our organizations is more comfortable.

When "trust happens," ***ease of being*** permeates our organizations and us as well.

"How do we make trust happen and create that ease of being?"

We contemplate this question.

As we ponder it, we'll:

1. Find that **trust** has an "ineffable" quality. "You-know-it-when-you-see-it" or "don't-see-it." It's ineffable because it "co-appears" with self-trusting, trusting, trustworthiness, trust relationships, and trust structures. "Trust" has no independent existence.

2. Explore how these five dimensions of trust interact to create a sixth one, systemic trust.

3. Discover that trust's elusiveness dissipates once we understand its V + 1 perspectives.

4. Learn tools to think and talk about "trust" and how to experience and create it.

5. Discover that "trust" is a **skill,** and we can enhance our ability and capacity to operate out of each trust dimension.

6. Develop a **"moment-by-moment"** recognition of our "trust perspectives" and those of others as we interact.

7. Realize that trust is a **choice**, which is good news because, at each moment, we can get better at

choosing — to trust or not. In other words, we are **"free to choose."**

8. Make trust happen!

Developing Facilitation Concepts, Tools, and Activities

We presented the first version of our "Model T" at the Mid-Atlantic Facilitators Network (MAFN) 2018-2019 Workshop Series on May 31, 2019.

In August 2020, we shared an updated version with participants in workshops for Dr. Cynthia Pace's client, Northrop Grumman. Based on our presentation, her client asked her to include our trust concepts in the curriculum she was developing for them.

In September 2020, Dr. Jerome Paige shared the model with one of his study groups (Samyama Study Group). Based on those discussions, we expanded our model. We increased our dimensions of trust from four (mental, behavioral, relational, and structural) to five (individual trust.)

Our model originated in our organizational development initiative **"Purpose, Trust & Personal Responsibility."** We began this initiative in 2003, and it has three tenets:

- **Purpose**

  With a valid and articulated purpose, organizations can maintain their sure-footedness in periods of rapid change and ever-unfolding periods of "a new normalcy."

- **Trust**

  Fast-moving and change-focused organizations don't

have time for a lot of "second-guessing." Trust reduces second-guessing.

- **Personal Responsibility**

  A self-directed employee is committed to the organization as demonstrated by their open-mindedness and willingness to learn, ownership of their performance, and initiative and creativity to improve organizational outcomes.

Our *Reference Manual* develops the "trust" component of that initiative.

In our *Manual*, we compare our Model T with Paul Lencioni's Five Behaviors of a Cohesive Team®, Integro's trust model, along with other perspectives on trust. These models, plus the DiSC® Facilitation System, provide key concepts we use in our facilitation practice.

We map various concepts of trust to our Model T.

We invite you to add your favorite trust model or trust concepts to the mix.

Developing A Precise Vocabulary

"Trust" is an elusive concept.

Why?

People use the concept differently.

We provide our "trust glossary" to help keep track of trust's various meanings. *See Figure 1.*

Trust Dimensions/Perspectives			Trust Affirmations		Trust Experiences
I	Mental	Vulnerability-Based	Trusting	I'm trusting	I am able and willing to share my vulnerabilities.
II	Behavioral	Behavior-Based	Trustworthiness	I'm trustworthy	I have aligned my workplace behaviors with expected trust behaviors.
III	Relational	Relationship-Based	Trust Relationships	I'm engaged in trust relationships	I'm hearing, and someone is hearing me. I'm listening and someone is listening to me.
IV	Structural	Organizational Alignment-Based	Organizational Trust	My organization and I are in alignment	I'm working in an environment where my work expectations and those of my organization align. Also, a mutual desire exists for me to remain a part of the organization.
V	Individual	Self-Awareness-Based	Self-Trust	I'm self-trusting	I'm engaging in practices that deepen my awareness and understanding of who I am and am not, and I'm "showing up" in my organization with authenticity and agency.
VI (V+1)	Systemic	Reinforcing-Based	Reinforcing Trust	My organization reinforces "virtuous cycles" "positive trust feedback loops."	I'm working in an organization where the five dimensions create a "whole" that is greater than the sum of its parts, and where an ease of being pervades my work environment.

FIGURE 1 — *Source: Paige-Pace*

With this glossary, you'll be able to specify the type of "trust" being discussed. Then, as you engage in organizational trust conversations, everyone will be clear about their trust expectations and what it takes to meet them.

Since we see our *Reference Manual* as a tool to clarify "trust," we welcome you to create your glossary based on your research, practice, and experience.

In *Figure 2* below, we visually depict our V+1 "trust dimensions." We place "trust" in the center.

For us, this means "trust co-arises" or "co-disappears."

Its appearance or disappearance happens when one or more of the five dimensions of trust is present. The sixth (V+1) dimension is the interaction among the other five.

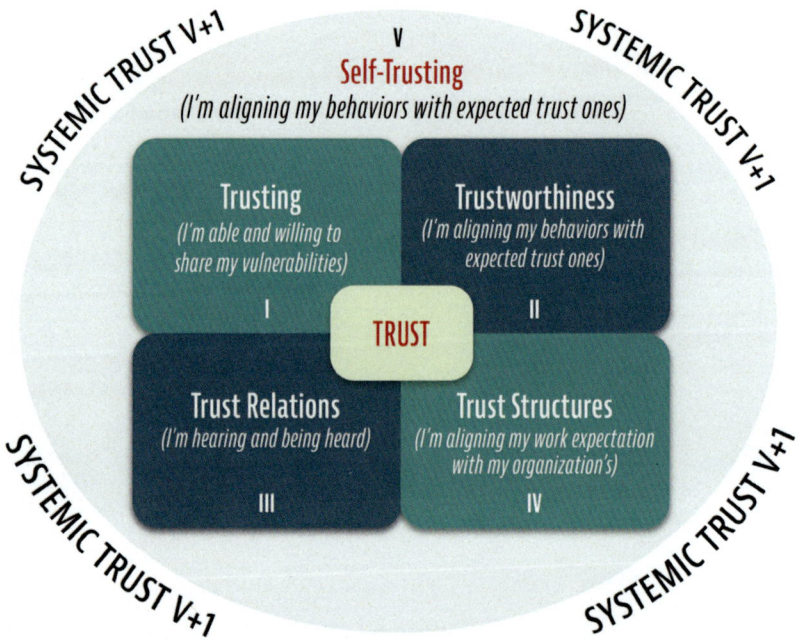

FIGURE 2 — *Source: Paige-Pace*

We give "self-trusting" a privileged position because a "stages model" undergirds our framework. *See Figure 3.*

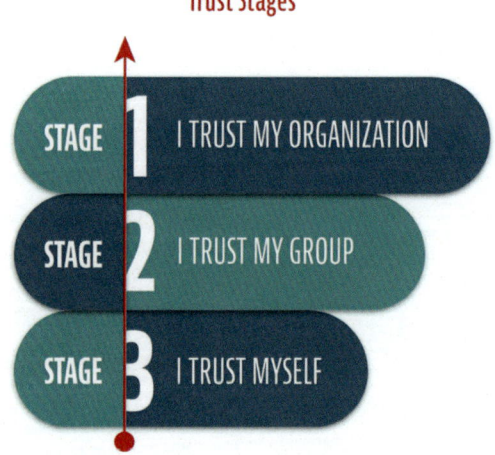

FIGURE 3 — *Source: Paige-Pace*

We begin with a "relationship with self."

We embrace the adage that all knowledge is self-knowledge. That is, we can only see in others what we see in ourselves. If we don't see something in ourselves, we can't see it in others.

We move from a relationship with self to relationships with others (our group) to relationships with our organizations (or institutions).

Holding "Trust Conversations"

Our *Reference Manual* offers tips on how to hold "trust conversations." It promotes "shared meaning." Shared meaning facilitates the discussion of the presence or absence of trust.

The "trust conversation" is also about being "trust-savvy."

What does that mean? We consciously operate within and among each of the "trust dimensions." That is, we develop a **moment-by-moment** recognition of our **trust perspectives** and those of others. We need to be aware of our perspectives when we're talking about trust.

For each dimension, we provide guided questions. As you answer these questions, you'll begin to operationalize each "trust perspective." *(See Appendix 1)*

Share Your "Making Trust Happen" Experiences

In our *Manual,* we:

1. Use the Five Behaviors of a Cohesive Team model by Paul Lencioni as a starting point to make our case that we need to clarify our use of the concept of "trust".

2. Lay the groundwork for our "Model T" based on five trust dimensions — vulnerability-based, behavior-based, relationship-based, structural-based, and self-awareness-based trust.

3. Suggest some "power questions" to explore the six perspectives of trust deeply. (Appendix 1)

4. Challenge us with "trust brain teasers." Think about "trust" as a ratio of "realizations" over "expectations." Check out Appendix 2. Let us know your answers.

Let's start a conversation about how to present and apply our Model T to answer the question: *"To Trust or Not to Trust?"*

As importantly, let's *"Make Trust Happen."*

We look forward to your feedback.

Jerome S. Paige

Cynthia O. Pace

Trust: An "Essential Quality"

What is "Trust?"

Take a moment and focus on the word in *Figure 4*.

- How do you define it?
- How do you use it? For example, what do you mean when you say you do or don't "trust" someone? Or the government? Or the Internet?
- What do you mean when you say you "trust" someone or something?

FIGURE 4 — *Source: Paige-Pace*

"Trust" is a problematic concept.

Why?

It doesn't have an "independent existence."

That means "trust" is an "essential quality." It's not separated from the conditions that give rise to it. In other words, "Trust Happens." It appears and disappears as conditions change.

What are the circumstances that cause "trust to happen?" For us, it's the interaction among trusting, trustworthiness, trust relationships, trust structures, and self-trust. *See Figure 5.*

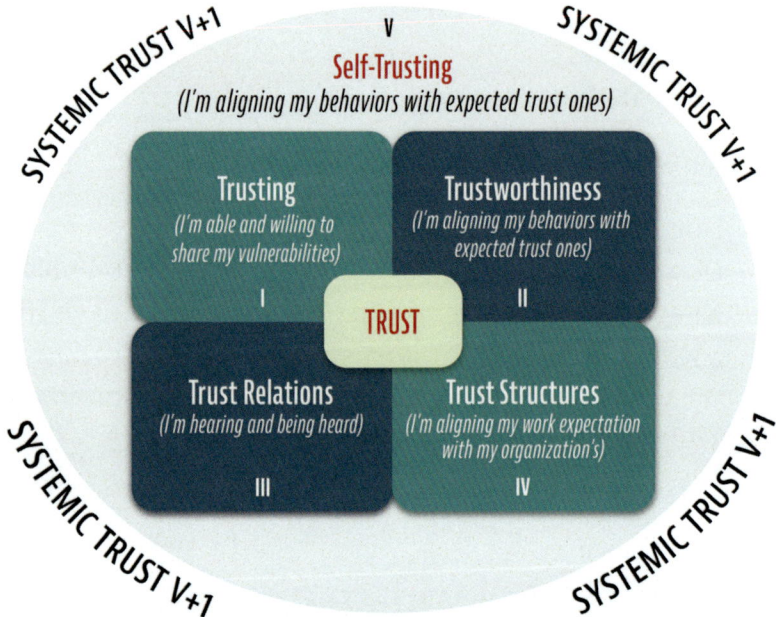

FIGURE 5 — *Source: Paige-Pace*

Since "trust" is an essential quality, we cannot define it.

Many others have difficulty defining trust as well. What happens is we talk about how "trust" manifests itself. We describe what life inside an organization is like when trust is present or absent. We rarely define it.

As an essential quality, trust falls under the adage: "We know it when we see it." Or "we recognize it by its absence."

Sometimes we define trust in psychological or mental terms. At other times, we use behavioral ones.

For example, Paul Lencioni's "Five Behaviors of a Cohesive Team"[1] uses a mental or emotional concept of trust. For him, this is the foundational behavior among a cohesive team's five behaviors.

10

We modify the Integral Vision Model framework[2] to identify uses and definitions of "trust." We identify five dimensions of trust."

1. Self-awareness
2. Mental
3. Behavioral
4. Relational
5. Structural

We also highlight how these dimensions interact to create a sixth — "systemic."

We "define" each "trust perspective."

- **Mental:** When I'm **trusting,** I am able and willing to share my vulnerabilities.
- **Behavioral:** When I'm **trustworthy,** I have aligned my workplace behaviors with expected trust behaviors.
- **Relational:** When I'm engaged in **trust relationships,** I'm hearing and am being heard. I'm listening, and someone is listening to me.
- **Structural:** When I'm experiencing **organizational trust,** an alignment exists between my expectations and my organization's. A mutual desire exists for me to remain a part of the organization.
- **Individual (Self):** When I'm **self-trusting,** I'm aware of and understand who I am. At work, I'm able to be authentic and express my agency.
- **Reinforcing: Reinforcing-based trust.** When my organization ensures a virtuous trust cycle (positive trust feedback loops.), I'm working in an environment where ease of being is pervasive.

As *Figure 5* above suggests, "trust happens." It co-arises. It appears along with something else. It never appears alone.

Five Dimensions of Trust

Trusting (Vulnerability-Based Trust)

This dimension focuses on an individual's willingness and ability to be "unguarded." The focus is a mental or emotional one.

As a **mental or psychological state,** "trust" comes and goes, and one's sense of it continually changes. *See Figure 6.*

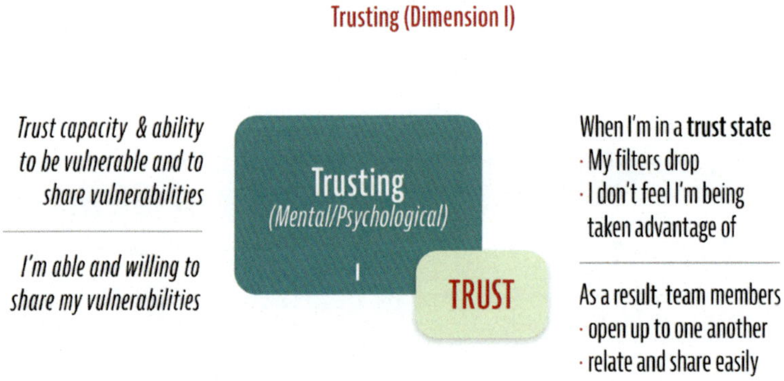

Trusting (Dimension I)

FIGURE 6 — *Source: Paige-Pace*

I'm unguarded at times; other times, I'm not.

When I'm in a **trust state,** I can drop my filters without feeling that someone will take advantage of me.

According to Lencioni, when "trust" is present, I'm ready to be "vulnerable" and to share my "vulnerability." So too are my team members.

Consequently, we "open up." We're able to relate and share effortlessly. We're experiencing Lencioni's ***vulnerability-based trust.***

12

When "trust" is present, unnecessary barriers have fallen. Conversely, when it's absent, obstacles arise to prevent us from interacting frictionlessly.

We've noted the effects of "trust's" presence or absence. However, we haven't defined it. We've recognized we're able to engage in unguarded interactions when we're trusting.

When trusting, "trust" and "unguardedness" **co-arise.** I can't separate **trusting (trust states)** from the presence of **trust conditions.** Or from their absence.

Since states are fluid, the **anticipation of trust** (or not trusting) develops. We're constantly on alert. We keep asking ourselves: "Should I trust, or not?"

"Trust" then is also a **state of readiness** (trust readiness).

This state allows us to be vulnerable around others[3]. Or not. Therefore, my **trust experiences** (trust memories) prepare me to trust under some circumstances. And not under others. Thus, **trust memories** and **trust readiness co-appear** as well.

Because we accumulate **trust experiences,** we have a **trust capacity** or **ability**[4]. Or inability. "Trusting" evolves through stages. We can get better at sharing our vulnerabilities.

Here, we get close to an affirmative operational definition of "trust:" *Trusting is the capacity and ability to be vulnerable and share vulnerabilities.*

We have **trust needs.** When we are fulfilling our needs, we feel comfortable sharing our vulnerabilities. Conversely, if we sense our **trust needs** are unmet, we won't open up.

Also, within the DiSC® Model, there are **trust types.** Varying conditions must be present for each style to trust fully[5].

Again, what under girds "trusting?" Trust experiences, anticipation, readiness, capacity, ability, needs, and types.

When I'm **trusting,** *I'm able and willing to share my vulnerabilities.*

Lencioni places "vulnerability-based trust" at the base of a cohesive team's five behaviors pyramid. It's the first of the five behaviors. And the most important one. *See Figure 7.*

Paul Lencioni's Five Behaviors Pyramid

FIGURE 7 — *Source: "Five Behaviors of a Cohesive Team," Wiley Publishing*

In our practice, we've also used the Strategic Alignment Survey published by Integro[6]. One "SAS behavior" is "openness." We've mapped that "behavior" to Trust Dimension-I. The mental/psychological perspective. *See Figure 8.*

C.O.A.R. (Openness)

Trusting (Vulnerability-Based Trust)

Employees
- Openly share information and opinions
- Discuss feelings with one another
- Do not withhold relevant information from one another

FIGURE 8 — *Source: Integro Strategic Alignment Survey (SAS)*

The other three SAS behaviors are congruence, acceptance, and reliability.

Our definition of "trusting" — I'm able and willing to share my vulnerabilities — is an important operational definition even though this definition doesn't address trust's indefinableness.

Lencioni's model provides useful tools for team members to improve at trusting. First, team members begin to understand they are more than disparate individuals. Then "trusting" becomes the cohesive agent that binds them together.

Trustworthiness (Behavior-Based Trust)

"Trusting" is a psychological concept.

"Trustworthiness" is a behavioral one.

Within Lencioni's framework, this aspect of "trust" relates to a team member's performance and competency. I "trust" someone if their behavior is predictable and reliable.

If I'm willing to put oneself in a **vulnerable** position, it must be because I have **confidence** in others. In behavioral economics, the primary determinant of trust is trustworthiness[7].

To assess behavioral trust (trustworthiness), we often rely on **reputation**. People are doing what they say they'll do.

Another way to assess **trustworthiness** is social distance. The shorter the "social distance," the higher the chance of observing trusting **attitudes** and **behaviors**, writes C. Monica Capra, Ph.D.[8] "Distance" can be psychological or physical.

We map two of the four "SAS behaviors" "congruency and reliability" to trustworthiness. *See Figure 9.*

C.O.A.R. (Congruence & Reliability)

Trustworthiness (Behavior-Based Trust)

CONGRUENCY

Employees
- Have clearly defined and agreed behavioral standards
- Make sure expectations are clear
- Are willing to discuss and resolve disagreements
- Practice what they preach

RELIABILITY

Employees
- Can rely on each other to get the job done
- Do what they say they will do
- Take ownership of their jobs
- Have high standards of quality in everything they do

FIGURE 9 — *Source: Intego Strategic Alignment Survey (SAS)*

Here the definition of trust relates to expected behaviors. *See Figure 10.*

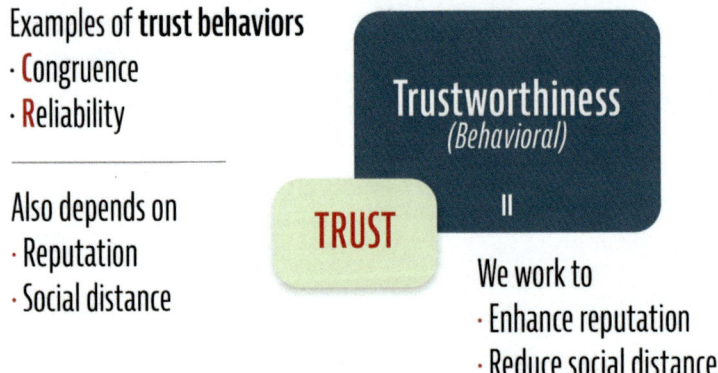

Trustworthiness (Dimension II)

I trust someone if their behavior is predictable and reliable

Examples of **trust behaviors**
· Congruence
· Reliability

Also depends on
· Reputation
· Social distance

Trustworthiness
(Behavioral)

II

TRUST

We work to
· Enhance reputation
· Reduce social distance

I've aligned my behaviors with expected trust behaviors

FIGURE 10 — *Source: Paige-Pace*

Two other behaviors in Lencioni's model correlate with "trust behaviors." They are **commitment** (buying in) and **accountability** (team members holding each other accountable.)

When I'm **trustworthy**, *I've aligned my behaviors with expected trust behaviors.*

With this operational definition of trust, we can learn "to trust." We can modify our trust behaviors like we can adjust any behavior.

Team members can learn to be trustworthy. They can learn how to behave in ways that bring them closer together.

Applying his model, we help team members transform a group of "I's" into a "We."

Team members can enhance their "reputation."

"Trustworthiness and performance" co-arise.

Trust Relationships (Relationship-Based Trust)

"Trusting" is a psychological concept.

"Trustworthiness" is a behavioral one.

"Trust relationships" provide an interpersonal approach to trust.

According to Lencioni, when trust is present, people aren't afraid to discuss issues. They are willing to engage in passionate dialogue around them. As a result, they engage in *"productive conflict."*

When "trust" is present, people don't hesitate to disagree with, challenge, or question one another to find the best answers, says Lencioni.

The SAS behavior *"acceptance"* maps to "relationship trust." *See Figure 11.*

SAS Behavior "Acceptance"

C.O.A.R. (Acceptance)

Trust Relationships (Relationship-Based Trust)

Employees
- Are really listened to
- Are accepted for who they are
- Feel safe express conflicting views
- Encourage and support each other

FIGURE 11 — *Source: Integro Strategic Alignment Survey (SAS)*

For us, **"relationship trust"** rests on two fundamental skills.

1. How to talk
2. How to listen.

Hence, we approach **"productive conflict"** through the dimension of **relationship-based trust**. We focus on focusing on "giving and receiving feedback." *See Figure 12.*

Trust Relationships (Dimension III)

Two fundamental skills:
· How to talk (give feedback)
· How to listen (receive feedback)

"Trust ability" can be enhanced. **Trust behaviors** can be learned — which means **trust relationships** can be built & enhanced.

TRUST

Trust Relationships
(Relational)

III

I'm hearing and being heard

FIGURE 12 — *Source: Paige-Pace*

As we enhance these skills, conversations become more productive. What's a "productive conversation?" At the end of it, we have:

- Shared information
- Gained mutual understanding
- Implemented processes to bring closure, and
- Created new possibilities for action.

We've given and received feedback

We equate "talking" with giving feedback and "listening" to receiving it.

What is "talking?"

>*It's using non-threatening language to share the effects of workplace behaviors on ourselves, others, and our organization.*

What is "listening?"

>*It's "the ability to receive and interpret verbal messages and other cues, like body language, to respond in ways that are appropriate to the purposes."*

Talking and listening involve understanding:

- How our "filters" shape how we receive information
- How we set our "filters" aside to hear and accept messages

"Trust relationships" combine aspects of trust states and behaviors. We can enhance "trust-ability." We can learn trust behaviors. In other words, we can build and improve "trust relationships."

When I'm engaged in trust relationships, I'm hearing, and someone is hearing me. I'm listening, and someone is listening to me.

Trust and trust relationships co-appear like "trustworthiness and performance" and "trusting and conditions." Mutual confidence is present, as well[9].

Like our other operational definitions, we can learn how to give and receive feedback. When we're better able to hear and be heard, ease of being will pervade our relationships.

We can:

- Build trust relationships
- Learn how to engage in "productive conflict"

- Create a well-integrated group of individuals
- Become a team.

Trust Structures (Organizational Alignment-Based Trust)

Trusting is a psychological concept.

Trustworthiness is a behavioral one.

Trust relationships provide an interpersonal approach.

A structural or systems idea of trust is an expectational trust.

Our organizations must continuously revalidate their existence. Why? Societal needs change. Ways to meet those needs are in constant flux, as well.

It's easier for employees "to buy in" (be committed), hold each other accountable, and focus less on the individual and more on organizational results when leaders state clearly and share the corporate vision and mission statements widely.

Furthermore, in today's era of an ever-changing normal, an organization's internal rate of change must equal or exceed its external one. Otherwise, an organization will lose its meaning.

Consequently, role clarity and an overall governing framework are key aspects of organizational trust.

Organizational alignment-based trust "co-arises." When?

When employees and stakeholders concur on the organization's direction, are engaged in collective decision-making, and jointly implement the company's mission. *See Figure 13.*

Trust Structure (Dimension IV)

I'm working in an environment where my work expectations and those of my organization align, and a mutual desire exists for me to remain a part of the organization.

"Alignment trust" that appears when employees, managers, leaders & stakeholders
· Concur on the direction of the organization,
· Are engaged in collective decision making,
· Participate jointly in the implementation of the mission

Roles and responsibilities clarified
· Shared shared direction
    — Collective decision-making
    — Joint implementation

TRUST

Trust Structures
(I'm aligning my work expectation with my organization's)

IV

FIGURE 13 — *Source: Paige-Pace*

When I'm experiencing organizational trust, I'm working in an environment where my work expectations and my organization's expectations align. As a result, a mutual desire exists for me to remain a part of the organization.

Organizational alignment trust links Lencioni's commitment and accountability behaviors.

When an organization is successful, there's buy-in to articulated rules, regulations, and governing frameworks.

According to Lencioni, once there's buy-in, it's easier for team members to hold each other accountable.

As with our other dimensions of trust, we have tools to align employee and organizational expectations.

"Alignment" is crucial to transforming a group of individuals into a high-performing team.

Furthermore, the more "organizational alignment trust" is present, the likelier mental, relationship, and behavioral trust will appear as well.

Self-Trust (Self-Awareness-Based Trust)

Self-trust is an "awareness" concept of "trust."

When I'm self-trusting, I'm engaging in practices that deepen my awareness of who I am.

- I have a deepened understanding of what I'm not.
- I know what it means to be authentic.
- I show up with "agency."

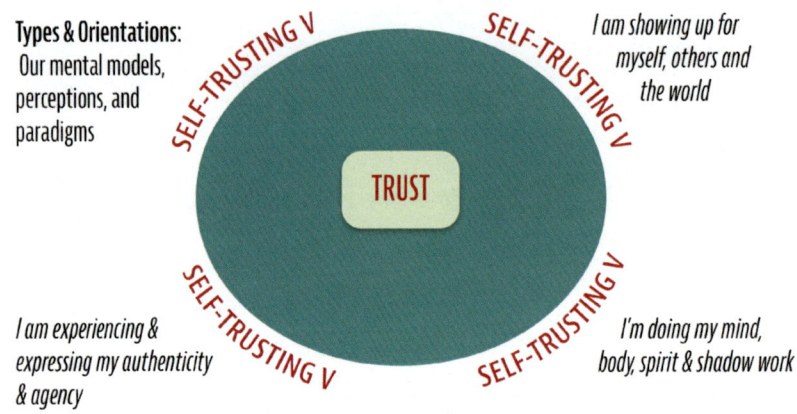

Figure 14 — *Source: Paige-Pace*

There's no correlate for "self-trust" in Lencioni's model. However, as we shared our model, we felt it was essential to add it. "Authenticity" is distinctive from "sharing stories with co-workers." Sharing stories is about getting to know each other better.

What is "self-trusting?"

- It's a form of individual internal structural alignment.

  The greater the alignment, the more likely a team member can expand their "trust capacity" and enhance their "trust-ability."

- What's the basis of this type of trust?

  It's the extent to which we can be "true to ourselves."

- It focuses us on looking inside.

  It forms a foundation for the other trust dimensions.

The extent we can "open up" to ourselves, the easier it will be for us to show up authentically for others.

Self-trusting and authenticity co-arise.

Systemic Trust (Dimension V+1)

Let's recap

Our V+1 dimensions:

- *Mental: A state of readiness or capacity* for "unguarded interaction." We can develop, expand, and nurture this capability.

- *Behavioral: An outcome* resulting from aligning work-place behaviors with trust ones. These behaviors are straightforwardness, openness, acceptance, and reliability.

- *Relational: A relationship of "mutual confidence"* in contractual performance. There is "honest" communication and expected competence. We can increase performance, open communication, and competence[10].

- **Structural:** *An organizational trust structure* promotes the clarification of roles and responsibilities. It leads to a shared direction, collective decision-making, and joint implementation.

- **Awareness:** *A self-awareness trust* deepens our insight into who we are. That awareness guides our organizational interactions.

Out of the interaction among these five elements, **Trust Happens.** *See Figure 15.*

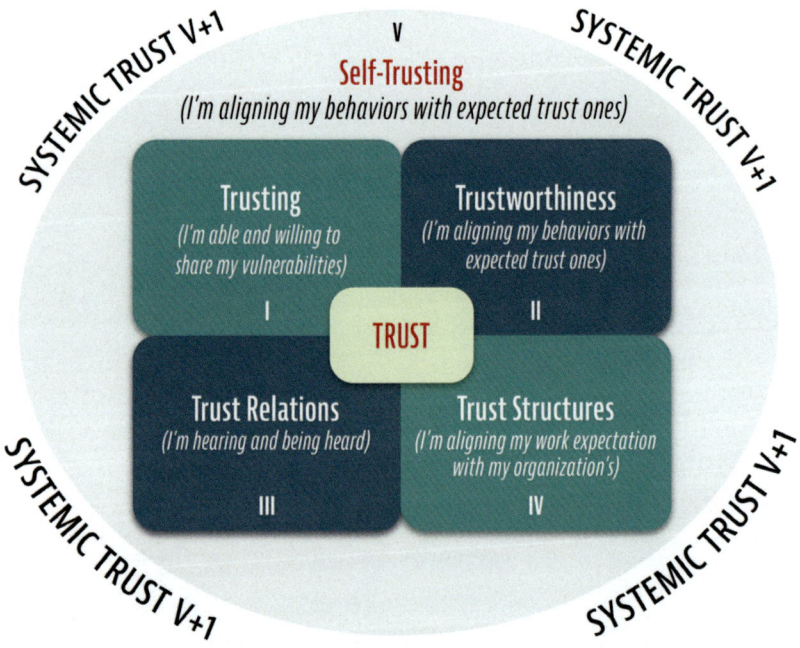

FIGURE 15 — *Source: Paige-Pace*

- **Reenforcing: Reenforcing-based trust** ensures **systemic trust.** It creates positive trust feedback loops. For example, I'm working in an organization where ease of being pervades me and my work environment. In other words, ***the whole is greater than the sum of its parts.*** A virtuous organizational cycle reinforces positive trust outcomes. A vicious cycle produces negative ones. *See Figure 15.*

Trust behaviors, relationships, and structures keep an organization running smoothly like a well-oiled machine. Monitor it consistently. Maintain it regularly.

Stages & Co-Arising Models

In a **co-arising model**, trust happens when one or more trust dimensions appear. Here, when we say that trust is present or absent, we're talking about the presence or absence of one of the trust perspectives. For example, *see Figure 16.*

Trust Co-Arising With Trusting

I have the capacity to be vulnerable. But I consciously choose to stay guarded. Some of my colleagues have no idea what it means to remover their blindfolds or to let down their guard. However, the more I and others are willing to be vulnerable, the more "trust" will become visible.

FIGURE 16 — *Source: Paige-Pace*

In a **stages model**, each level builds on the previous one. An example of this is Lencioni's Five Behaviors Pyramid. (See *Figure 7 above.*) Synonyms for stages are ladders, stairs, and maturity. For example, one view of our Model-T as a stages model appears in *Figure 17* below. In this array, the foundation is "self-trust," We move through stages to reach systemic trust.

Model T As A Stages Model

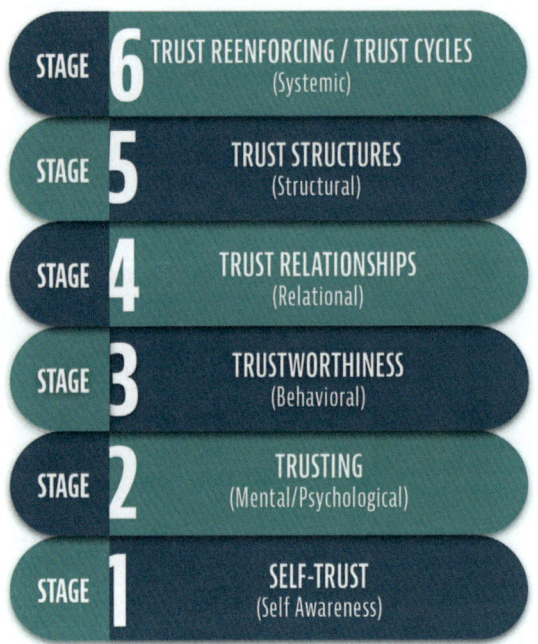

STAGE **6** TRUST REENFORCING / TRUST CYCLES
(Systemic)

STAGE **5** TRUST STRUCTURES
(Structural)

STAGE **4** TRUST RELATIONSHIPS
(Relational)

STAGE **3** TRUSTWORTHINESS
(Behavioral)

STAGE **2** TRUSTING
(Mental/Psychological)

STAGE **1** SELF-TRUST
(Self Awareness)

FIGURE 17 — *Source: Paige-Pace*

Based on your organization and experience, you can stack "the stages" differently. The array of the dimensions of trust into the stages in *Figure 17* is suggestive, not prescriptive.

The game "Jenga" illustrates the importance of the array of the building blocks and what happens when blocks are absent or removed. *See Figure 18 below.*

Model T Without All the Building Blocks

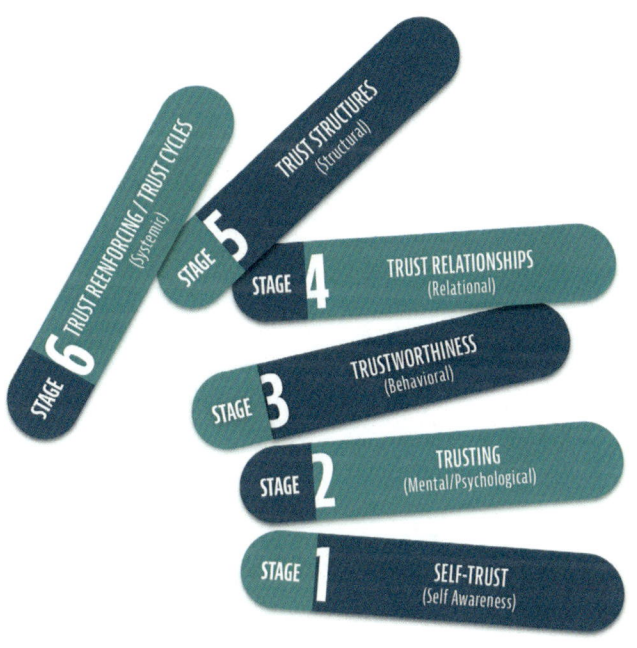

FIGURE 18 — *Source: Paige-Pace*

The Importance of Trust

(Virtuous & Vicious Organizational Trust Cycles)

Trust Strengthens Relationships

Trust is the greatest asset in a complex system like an organization.

Its survival requires a total engagement of the whole system's elements. An organization requires abundant information that must flow seamlessly through current and new channels.

Organizational boundaries are malleable. Metaphorically speaking, we never step into the same river twice. A perpetual newness and a need for ongoing renewal require collaboration, participation, openness, and inclusion.

"Trust happening" across the five and within the V+1 dimension enhances relationships.

Trust Eliminates Second Guessing

Trust is the glue that holds an organization together.

Fast-moving and change-focused organizations don't have time for a lot of second-guessing.

Trust helps eliminate second-guessing.

In today's organizations, employees must be able to perform with minimal guidance. They need to value and express autonomy without concern about their needs being met or intentionally undermined. As Rob Lebow and Randy Spitzer outline in their book on accountability, "trust" allows for "freedom and responsibility without control." Trust helps top-down, hierarchical forms of organizational regulation give way to a bottom-up, self-regulation approach[11].

Employees are self-trusting, and they are aware of how the other dimensions of trust unfold in their organizations. Organizations with positive trust feedback loops attract and retain trustworthy employees. There's less internal organizational friction. Employees and the organization will be better able to adapt to an ever-present "new normal." And to thrive in their ever-changing environment.

Trust Makes Life Easier

Everything is more relaxed and more comfortable to achieve.

According to Heathfield, "When trust exists in an organization or a relationship, almost everything else is easier and more comfortable to achieve[12]."

How do we interpret her statement within our Model-T?

When trust co-disappears, employees tend to dis-engage. They become other, rather than self-directed. They experience their work environments as being unpleasant. Alternatively, when trust co-appears, a pleasant work environment co-arises as well.

Making Trust Happen!

Trust is a choice, as well as a skill.

"Trust" arises from the interaction among several dimensions mind, brain, behavior, relationships, and structures. We've suggested that each element carries its manifestation of "trust." No universal definition of "trust" exists. "Trust" is a byproduct of several ingredients coming together. Thus, the whole of trust is greater than the sum of its parts.

Take, for example, a "movement network[13]."

This type of network is a group of organizations that coalesces around an issue. Why? Because the organizations have shared interests and goals. They collaborate to address complex problems. They focus on "cross or "single-issues." They have a common goal. That is, "the transformation of power relationships" in society.

Network leaders bring "trust" into being by:

- Building and investing in relationships
- Modeling personal integrity
- Valuing what each network member brings to the table
- Ensuring transparency and accountability, and
- Employing clear, straightforward, accessible communications.

Once we understand trust's dimensions, we realize that trust is a choice. It's a skill as well.

We can improve our ability to make wise trust choices. We can enhance our capacity.

At each moment, we can get better at choosing "to trust." In other words, we are **free to choose** or not.

As important, we can *make trust happen!*

When it *happens:*

- Relationships among team members strengthen
- Second-guessing dissipates, and
- Organizational life is more comfortable and productive.

Appendix 1
Trust Inquiries

Power Questions And The V+1 Dimensions of Trust

This section presents questions to explore each of the V +1 trust dimensions. *See Figure 19.* We recast this familiar term, trust, until it demands an explanation.

Mapping Power Question to the V+1 Dimension of Trust

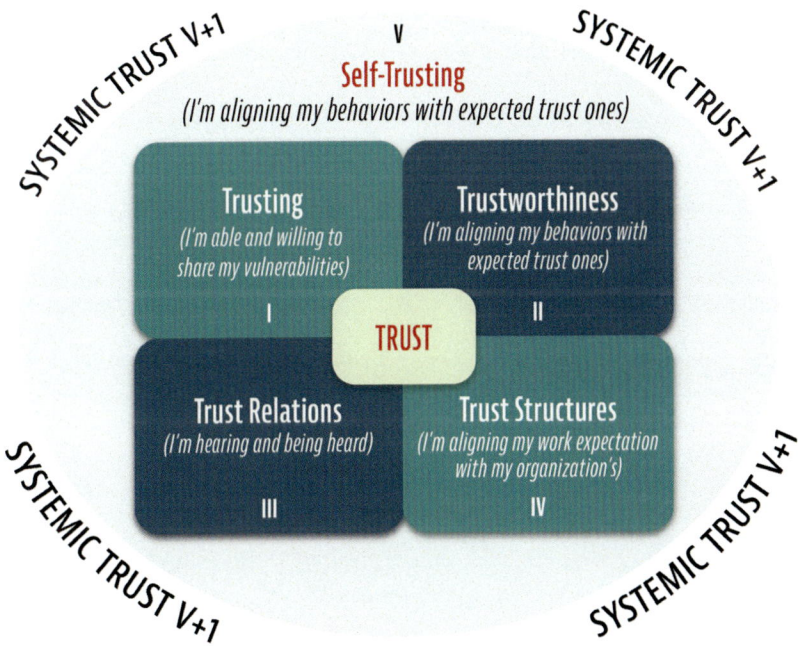

FIGURE 19 — *Source: Paige-Pace*

We present a three-stage model.

Stage 1 is the current trust condition.

Stage 3 is the desired condition.

Stage 2 is a transitional one. It takes us from the "as-is" to "to-be" conditions — from the "current" to "desired" conditions. We provide a stages model for each dimension in *Figure 19. See Figure 20.*

Making Trust Happen

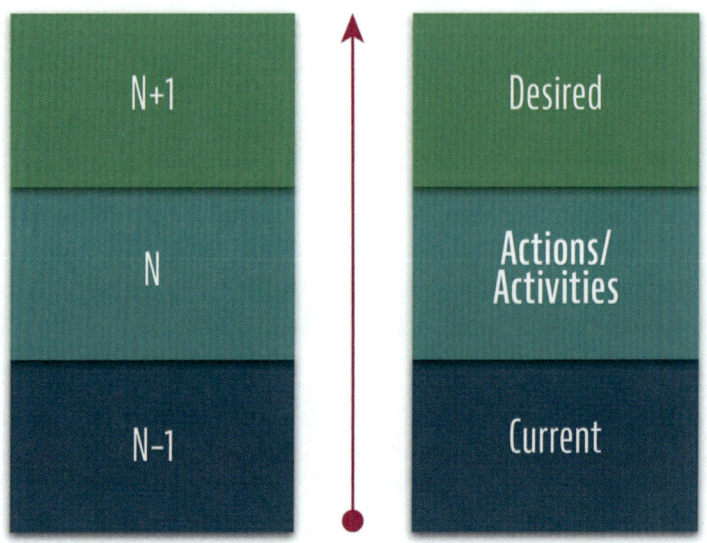

FIGURE 20 — *Source: Paige-Pace*

Groups and individuals periodically experience a gap between their current (as-is) and desired (to-be) states — between a "non-trust" and a "trust" condition.

What will it take to "close the gap?"

1. Understand each stage's characteristics
2. Identify the actions that will move us from the "as-is" to the "to-be" stage.

The key to our approach to close the gap is "The Power

Question (PQ)."

We use "power questions (PQ's)" to guide inquiry.

The field of facilitation abounds with "inquiry methods." There are models like "appreciative inquiry" and "world cafes."

For us, as our workshop participants contemplate the PQ's, they move from deepened reflections to expanded understanding to enhanced appreciation to personal transformation. *See Figure 21.*

From Question To Transformation

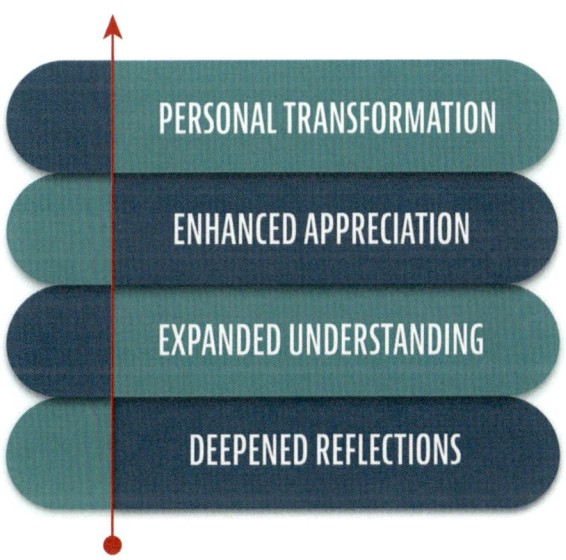

FIGURE 21 — *Source: Paige-Pace*

We can measure the progress by using a pre/post-assessment.

What is personal transformation?

- The familiar has been restated.
- Perspectives have shifted.
- A "light" has come on.

- It's like: "Oh. Now I see."

Our PQ's take us beyond a simple "yes or no" answer. We use them to help clients explore their current and desired states. They help participants identify actions to take to "close the gap."

We also emphasize there's no end to the process

Tomorrow's "to-be" stage will eventually become today's "as-is" one."

That's because we live in a dynamic environment. There will always be an "N+1 Stage." Organizations and individuals are always "in transition." We continuously face an unfolding "new normal."

As part of the organizational development services we offer, we facilitate transitions from "current to desired" states.

Power Questions: Making Vulnerability-Based Trust Happen

Purpose of the Power Questions

Being "vulnerable" means you can be "unguarded." These questions help identify the barriers to experiencing "vulnerability-based" trust. They uncover the conditions needed for team members to engage in "trusting" in the workplace. **(Anticipation & Openness)**

Power Questions

- What keeps you from sharing something personal with your co-workers?
- What do you experience in your body/mind when you can't share?
- How do you feel when you can share?

- What must be in place or happen so you can move from a guarded to an unguarded state?

Guided Questions

- Describe a workplace situation when you were "unguarded."
- What types of physical and emotional states or sensations did you experience?
- How would you describe your interactions with colleagues?
- Describe a workplace situation where you had to be "guarded" all the time.
- What types of physical and emotional states or sensations did you experience?
- How would you characterize your interactions with colleagues?

Figure 22 maps the process of going from "non-vulnerable" to "vulnerable."

To-Be	Unguarded	*I am **able** and **willing** to share my vulnerabilities*
Transitions/ Actions/Activities	Personal Stories/Sharing	Personal Stories/Sharing
As-Is	Guarded	*I am **unable** and **unwilling** to share my vulnerabilities*

1. Describe the characteristics of the as-is state.
2. Describe the characteristics of the to-be state.
3. Indicate what it will take to move from one state to the next.
4. Describe what happens during the "transition."
5. Design an activity that will help in making the transition.

Assessment Tools:
· DiSC
· 5B's

FIGURE 22 — *Source: Paige-Pace*

Note: We all have a "persona" or" a public face." We're human. That's normal. However, when we're able to share something personal, we take off our "masks." Someone now knows something about us they never knew before. Behind and beyond all the "roles," we all share common humanness.

Keep in mind that we're not striving for "true confessions." We're after knowing each other as human beings.

Contemplating the PQ's helps us experience each other "beyond our veils."

We start with "personal stories" because we know from several disciplines that "storytelling" is compelling and exciting. When we share our "stories," we're sharing ourselves. We're creating "safe spaces/places" to allow ourselves and others to be "human" as well.

Power Questions: Making Behavior-Based Trust Happen

Purpose of the Power Questions

"Behavior" is
- How we act
- What and how we write
- How we express and present ourselves.

We can get to know others by observing their behavior. They get to know us by watching ours[14].

The purpose of these questions is to explore how we develop trustworthiness in ourselves and others. **(Expectations & Performance)**

Power Questions

What behaviors do you or others exhibit that indicate "trustworthiness?"

- How do you define and experience "trustworthiness?"
- What actions cause you to see someone as "untrustworthy?"
- What would it look like? Describe it.

Guided Questions

- What are some other ways to describe:
  o "Trustworthiness?"
- What behaviors do others exhibit that:
  o Promote trustworthiness?
  o Undermine trustworthiness?

Figure 23 maps the process of going from being "non-trustworthy" to "trustworthy."

Making Behavior-Based Trust Happen

1. Describe the characteristics of the as-is state.
2. Describe the characteristics of the to-be state.
3. Indicate what it will take to move from one state to the next.
4. Describe what happens during the "transition."
5. Design an activity that will help in making the transition.

Assessment Tools:
- DiSC
- 5B's
- Strategic Alignment Survey

FIGURE 23 — *Source: Paige-Pace*

Power Questions: Making Relationship-Based Trust Happen

Purpose of the Power Question

During a workplace "conversation," we give and receive feedback. We are listening. Someone is listening to us.

At the end of a conversation, we will have:

- Shared information
- Gained understanding
- Experienced a shift in perspective.

The purpose of these questions is to enhance our willingness and ability to speak and listen. **(Speaking & Listening)**

Power Question

What causes you to open up and share? What drives you to shut down and withhold?

Guided Questions

- What does it mean:
  - o "To talk?"
  - o "To listen?"

How do you currently

- Give feedback?
- Receive feedback?

Describe a conversation where you

- "Closed down." What was ongoing in your body?
- "Opened up." What was going on in your body?

How do you improve workplace communication?

Figure 24 maps the process of going from a state of "non-hearing/listening" to "hearing/listening."

To-Be	Open Communications	*I am* hearing and *am* being heard
Transitions/ Actions/Activities	Giving & Receiving Feedback	Giving & Receiving Feedback
As-Is	Closed Communications	*I am not* hearing and *am* not being heard

1. Describe the characteristics of the as-is state.
2. Describe the characteristics of the to-be state.
3. Indicate what it will take to move from one state to the next.
4. Describe what happens during the "transition."
5. Design an activity that will help in making the transition.

Assessment Tools:
· DiSC
· How to Speak. How To Listen (Communications)

FIGURE 24 — *Source: Paige-Pace*

Power Questions: Making Organizational Alignment-Based Trust Happen

Purpose of the Power Questions

"Alignment" refers to how an employee's values and goals relate to the values and goals of their organization. The purpose of these questions is to focus on "the employee-organizational fit." **(Individual & Organizational Purpose)**

Power Questions

- To what extent do your work expectations and the expectations of your organization align?

- To what extent does a mutual desire exist for you to remain a part of the organization?

42

Guided Questions

- Are organizational roles & responsibilities clear?
  - o Why?
  - o Why not?
- Are your goals and objectives aligned with your organization's?
  - o Why?
  - o Why not?
- To what extent are the following present in your organization
  - o Shared direction?
  - o Collective decision-making?
  - o Joint implementation?

Figure 25 maps the process of going from a state of "non-alignment" to "alignment."

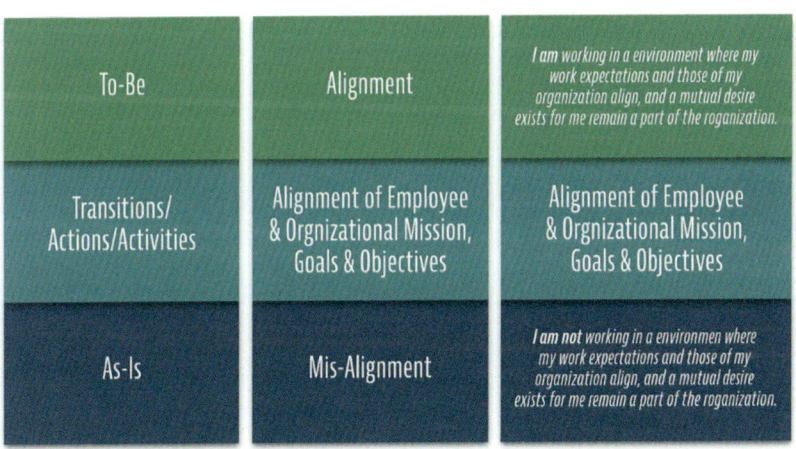

Making Organizational Alignment-Based Trust Happen

To-Be	Alignment	I am working in a environment where my work expectations and those of my organization align, and a mutual desire exists for me remain a part of the roganization.
Transitions/ Actions/Activities	Alignment of Employee & Orgnizational Mission, Goals & Objectives	Alignment of Employee & Orgnizational Mission, Goals & Objectives
As-Is	Mis-Alignment	I am not working in a environmen where my work expectations and those of my organization align, and a mutual desire exists for me remain a part of the roganization.

1. Describe the characteristics of the as-is state.
2. Describe the characteristics of the to-be state.
3. Indicate what it will take to move from one state to the next.
4. Describe what happens during the "transition."
5. Design an activity that will help in making the transition.

Assessment Tools:
- DiSC
- Workplace Expectations

FIGURE 25 — *Source: Paige-Pace*

Power Questions: Making Self-Awareness-Based Trust Happen

Purpose of the Guided Questions

I'm "self-aware" when I know who I am. When I "show up," I'm expressing my self-knowledge.

The purpose of these questions is to explore what it means "to live one's truth." **(Authenticity & Agency)**

Power Questions

What does it mean to you to "show up authentically" for yourself, others, and your organizations?

Guided Questions

- Are you true to yourself?
- How do you experience being honest and in alignment with your true self?
- Are your mind and gut in agreement?
- What's the link between your internal calm and
  o Giving & receiving feedback
  o Aligning your persona and your organization's goals

Figure 26 maps to the process of going from being "inauthentic" to "authentic."

Making Self-Awareness-Based Trust Happen

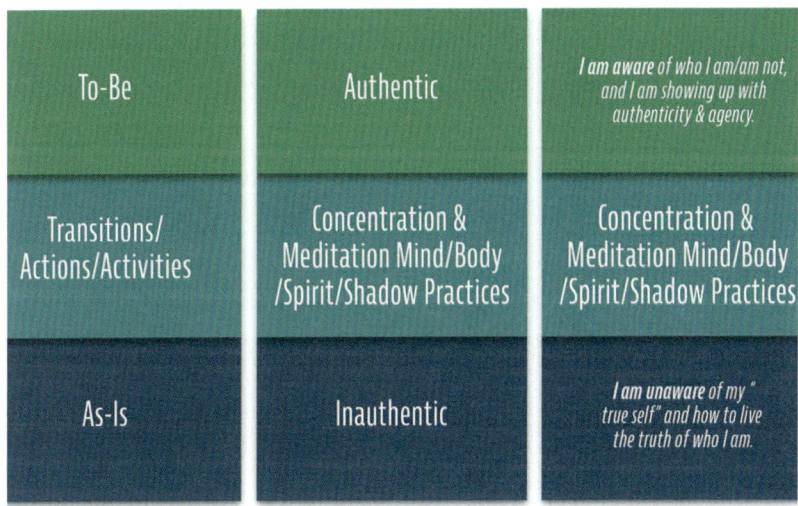

To-Be	Authentic	*I am aware of who I am/am not, and I am showing up with authenticity & agency.*
Transitions/ Actions/Activities	Concentration & Meditation Mind/Body /Spirit/Shadow Practices	Concentration & Meditation Mind/Body /Spirit/Shadow Practices
As-Is	Inauthentic	*I am unaware of my " true self" and how to live the truth of who I am.*

1. Describe the characteristics of the as-is state.
2. Describe the characteristics of the to-be state.
3. Indicate what it will take to move from one state to the next.
4. Describe what happens during the "transition."
5. Design an activity that will help in making the transition.

· Concentration & meditation practices

FIGURE 26 — *Source: Paige-Pace*

Power Questions: Making Reinforcing-Based Trust Happen

Purpose of the Guided Questions

The purpose of these questions is to explore what happens when the V+1 dimensions interact. Additionally, we'll examine how to enhance the interactions that create a virtuous cycle and avoid those that cause a vicious one. **(Virtuous & Vicious Cycles)**

Power Questions

A "virtuous cycle" reinforces positive outcomes. A "vicious cycle" creates negative ones. What would cause a virtuous cycle to unfold in your organization? In what ways would a vicious cycle play out?

Guided Questions

- Remove one of the dimensions -- individual, mental, behavioral, relational, and structural. How are the remaining ones affected?

  o How is "the whole" affected?

  o What are some warning signs that something might be amiss?

- What are the leading and lagging indicators to watch?
- Conversely, what are some warning signs that things are going along well?

Figure 27 maps the process of going from vicious to virtuous trust cycles.

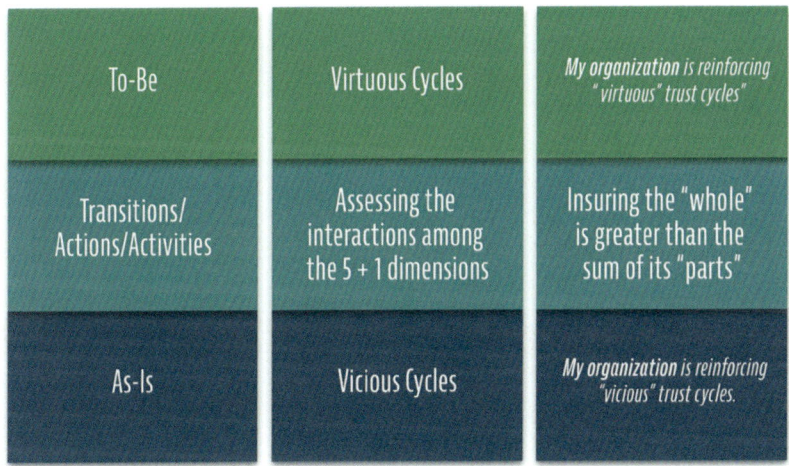

1. Describe the characteristics of the as-is state.
2. Describe the characteristics of the to-be state.
3. Indicate what it will take to move from one state to the next.
4. Describe what happens during the "transition."
5. Design an activity that will help in making the transition.

· Organizational Self-Study
· Strategic Alignment Surveys

FIGURE 27 — *Source: Paige-Pace*

Share with us your experiences driving our Model T. We welcome feedback. What modifications have you made? What ones would you'd like for us to make?

Appendix 2

Trust Ratios: A Simplification of "Trust"

A Path of Simplification

Many people.

Many definitions.

Yes. "Trust" means many things to different people.

In our Trust Model, we "simplify" what we mean when we say we "trust" someone or something. We recast the familiar until it demands explanation.

Our "path to simplification" unfolds as follows:

First: We take the many concepts of trust and divide them into six.

We express these six as "V + 1." The five are self-trusting, trusting, trustworthiness, trust relationships, and trust structures. Alternatively, they are individual awareness, mental/psychological, behavioral, relationships, structural. The sixth is reinforcing, or systemic.

Second: We discuss how interaction among these five components creates a whole greater than the sum of its parts. *See Figure 28.*

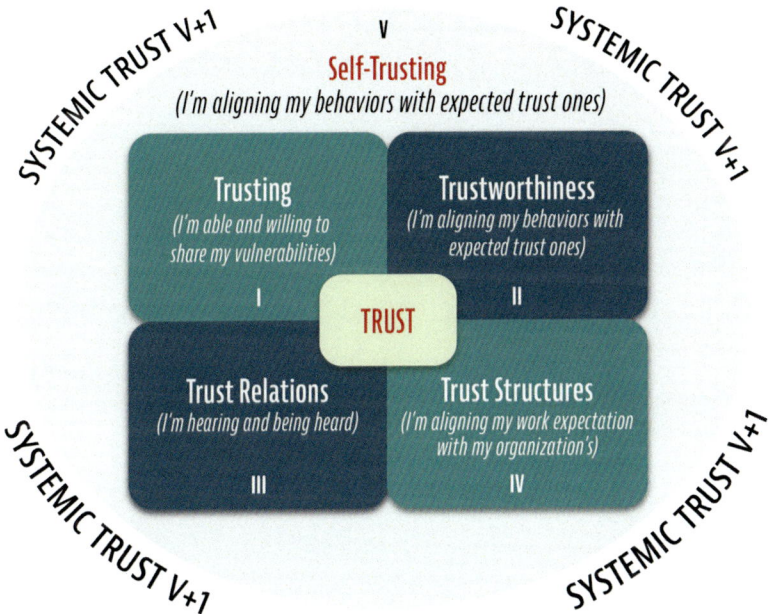

FIGURE 28 — *Source: Paige-Pace*

Third: We simplify these six into two — "trust realizations" and "trust expectations." *See Figure 29.*

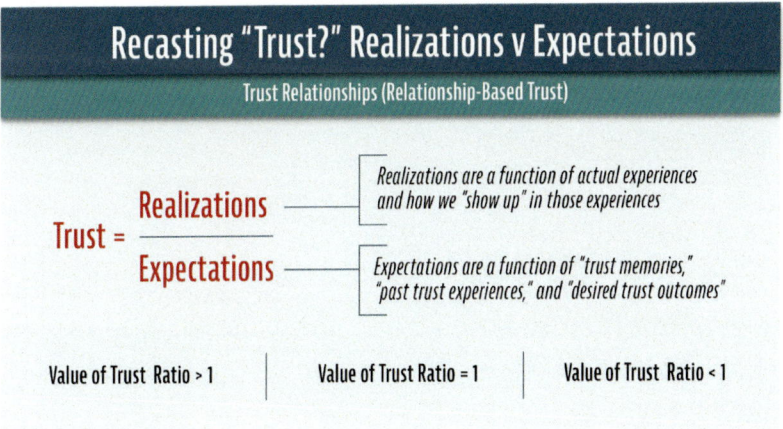

FIGURE 29 — *Source: Paige-Pace*

Fourth: We express "realizations" and "expectations" as a "ratio." We've gone from "many" concepts of trust to 6 to 5 to 2 to 1. It's a "1" because the 2" comprises a dyad. They aren't separate.

A Dyadic Relationship

What's a dyadic relationship? Think of the Yang-Yin symbol. Two interacting forces create the whole. Within biology, there's a positive and negative force. These forces keep the cell together. Without the two, the cell doesn't exist.

For our "Model T," as the relationship between "realizations" and "expectations" changes, the value of the trust ratio varies.

An example: If "realization" is on the top of the fraction and "expectation" is on the bottom, when "realization" is higher than "expectation," then the value of the trust ratio (VTR) is greater than one.

Here's a "trust brain teaser."

How would you explain the meaning of the trust ratio value for your organization?

- VTR=1
- VTR>1
- VTR<1

See Figure 26 above.

Take "vulnerability-based trust," for example, and explain what it means for your organization when VTR>1, VTR=1, and VTR<1?

Keep going!

What's the situation in your organization if "R=0" or "E=0?" Use "behavioral-based trust" as the example. Or try relationship-based, structural-based, or individual-based trust.

Power Questions — Again

These questions about the relationships between "realizations" and "expectations" are examples of Power Questions (PQ's)" discussed in Appendix 1. Again, PQ's guide inquiry.

Again, these types of questions take us beyond simple "yes or no" answers. They help workshop participants deepen their reflections, enhance their appreciation, engage in new experiences, and shift their perspectives. By contemplating PQ's, workshop participants move toward "transformation." *See Figure 30.*

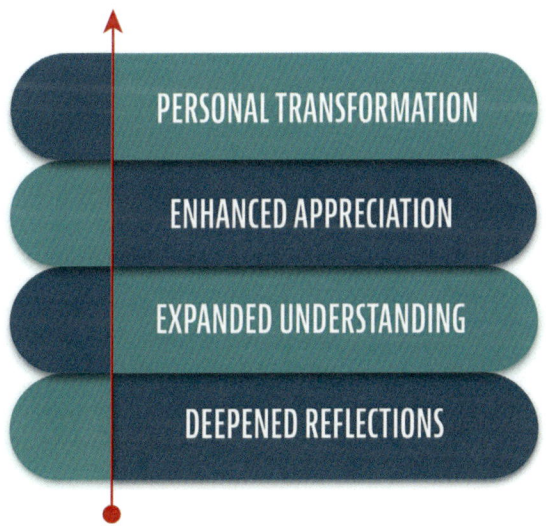

FIGURE 30 — *Source: Paige-Pace*

51

What is "transformation?" For our purposes, it's a shift in perspective. Workshop participants will "look at the world" differently. For us, that means that after the workshop, participants will be "trust-savvy." They will know why "trust" is ineffable and how to navigate its six dimensions to make it happen. We can assess their progress by using pre/post-assessments.

Trust Brain Teasers Power Questions

Below are additional "trust brain teasers."

Keep in mind our position: "Trust co-arises or co-disappears along with one or more of the dimensions of trust."

Experiment with each of the six dimensions of trust -- awareness, mental, behavioral, relational, structural, and systemic.

Craft a "story" about the value of your organization's "trust ratio." By value, we mean whether the organizational trust ratio is equal to, greater than, or less than one.

Using the characteristics of the six dimensions of trust, describe what's happening to your organization's "value of trust ratio" (VTR) when:

The values of (R) and (E) change in relationship to one another.

For example, "realization" (R) is rising faster than "expectation" (E)

- VTR is decreasing: (E) is increasing faster than (R)
- VTR=1 means E=R

What are the manifestations of these values in your organization?

What's your prediction about your organization's future when:

R=0 and E>1 (VTR= 0)
E=0 and R > 0
R=0 while E>1

Are these even possible in your organization?

Share your thoughts with us.

Endnotes

1 The Five Behaviors of a Cohesive Team Facilitation Kit, Wiley Publication.

2 Wilber, Ken; Patten, Terry; Leonard, Adam; and Morelli, Marco. Integral Life Practice; A 21st Century Blueprint for Physical Health, Emotional Balance, Mental Clarity and Spiritual Awakening. Boston: Integral Books, 2008.

3 Adapted from Dennis S. Reina & Michelle L. Reina "Trust and Betrayal in the Workplace" Building Effective Relationships in Your Organization. Berrett-Koehler Publishers; Third edition (February 2, 2015); Susan M. Heathfield "Trust Rules." Heathfield identifies three constructs of trust: a capacity for trusting, perception of competence, and the perception of intentions.

https://www.thebalancecareers.com/trust-rules-the-most-important-secret-about-trust-1919393 and the Integro, "Leadership Development Process"

4 Susan M. Heathfield, Trust Rules: When trust exists in an organization or a relationship, almost everything else is easier and more comfortable to achieve. In building on the work of Duane C. Tway, Jr.'s 1994 dissertation, A Construct of Trust, Heathfield identifies three constructs of trust: a capacity for trusting, perception of competence, and the perception of intentions.

https://www.thebalancecareers.com/trust-rules-the-most-important-secret-about-trust-1919393

5 "Everything DiSC Facilitation System," Wiley Publication

6 Integro, Leadership Development Process. We borrowed the concept of trust behaviors straightforwardness, openness, acceptance, and reliability from this model. See https://www.integroleadership.com. As we apply our model, we continuously modify how we define each of these behaviors.

7 "At its heart, trust is about making a choice: Do I rely on this person, or do I not. Having trust means that you're willing to enter into a risky situation with another person because you believe in them. Trust is needed in situations where working with someone is better than working alone. But, working with someone brings risks: what if that person lets me down, or what if they prove to be unreliable." Benjamin Ho. Why Trust Matters: An Economist's Guide to the Ties That Bind Us. Columbia University Press (June 29, 2021)

8 "What do we know about trust?" https://www.behavioraleconomics.com/what-do-we-know-about-trust/ (last visited 7/27/2021)

9 See: "Construct Of Trust" by Duane Converse, Jr., Bs, Ms. Dissertation. Presented To The Faculty Of The Graduate School Of The University Of Texas At Austin In Partial Fulfillment Of The Requirements For The Degree Of Doctor Of Philosophy The University Of Texas At Austin May 1994

10 Adapted from Dennis S. Reina & Michelle L. Reina "Trust and Betrayal in the Workplace"; Susan M. Heathfield "Trust Rules," and Integro, "Leadership Development Process"

11 Rob Lebow and Randy Spitzer (2002). "Accountability; Freedom and Responsibility without Control." Barrett-Koehler: San Francisco.

12 Heathfield above in Footnote 4

13 Mark Leach and Laurie Mazur. Creating Culture: Promising Practices of Successful Movement Networks. The Nonprofit Quarterly. Fall/Winter 2013. www.npqmag.org

14 This is the concept of "behavior" that is key to the "DiSC Facilitation System." We focus on what we can "observe."

About Jerome S. Paige & Cynthia O. Pace

DR. JEROME S. PAIGE is an economics, business, and organizational consultant, with over 40 years of experience in higher education, public sector, and non-profit organizations. He holds a master's and a doctorate in economics from the American University and a B.A. degree in economics from Howard University. He is the principal in his firm, Jerome S. Paige &Associates, LLC. Dr. Paige is a Five Behaviors of Cohesive Team® Authorized Partner, and a DiSC® Certified Trainer. He is also a trained meditation instructor in the tradition of iRest® (Integrative Restoration) and offers meditation workshops.

Jerome S. Paige & Associates provides organizational consulting services include strategic planning, business development, performance measurement & management, and change management. Since we bring a fresh perspective to organizational performance, we provide leaders and managers with clear and easily graspable concepts to ensure their organizations are mission-driven, opportunity-seeking, outcomes-based, and results-oriented.

A key focus of our organizational consulting work is "trust." Fast-moving and change-focused organizations don't have time for second-guessing, and since trust helps eliminate second-guessing, it's the cohesive that holds an organization together.

www.whatsonjeromesmind.com
www.paigeandassociates.com

DR. CYNTHIA PACE is the Founder and Senior Partner of PACE-MAKER, LLC, Chair of the Mid Atlantic Facilitators Network, and the former U.S. Director of the International Association of Facilitators.

She is also a certified professional facilitator endorsed by the International Association of Facilitation™ (CPF, an author, keynote speaker, and project manager of leading teams.

Clients engage her and the PACE-MAKER associates when they want their organization and employees to embrace a culture of trust and personal responsibility, turning an irregular organizational heartbeat into a drumbeat-a jungle into a garden. Her leadership/group facilitation practice and events electrify the organization's pulse by uncovering its intrinsic wiring from top to bottom.

She has declared war on meetings, retreats, and business sessions that produce less than optimal results, turning business boredom into meeting magic.

Unlike most, she offers the client the opportunity to experience real-time leadership — an experience that is memor-able, penetrat-able, and remark-able. She is internationally known for her dynamic presentations and creative project management. She tells it like it is. Her clients describe her as energizing, fun-filled, and enlightening.

www.leadershipguru.com

Making Trust Happen

1. **Explain**

   Ensure everyone shares the same meaning of "trust."
   Use the definitions (dimensions) in our "trust glossary"
   or others. Our model is suggestive, not prescriptive.

2. **Examine**

   Determine everyone's current (as-is) and desired (to-
   be) trust levels (stages). Use surveys, guided inquiries
   (power questions), or "trust" exercises.

3. **Engage**

   Use activities that move everyone from their current
   to desired trust level. For example, increase everyone's
   ease at giving and receiving feedback.

4. **Expand**

   Enhance everyone's "trust-ability." Why? Their "to-be"
   stage will become their current "as-is" one. Organizations
   are constantly in flux. For everyone, there will always
   be an "N+1 Trust Stage" to attain.